Mountain Mutts

Joy's Tale

Mountain Mutts – Joy's Tale
© Copyright, 2021 by Julie Stephens
All rights reserved.
Hands Be Strong, Inc.

9 8 7 6 5 4 3

Third Printing January 2023

ISBN: 978-0-9742680-5-7

Printed in the United States of America

Mountain Mutts – Joy's Tale
Copyright Registration Number TX0009055979 / May 21, 2021

For our beloved children
David and Elizabeth
and dog lovers everywhere.

"God will prepare everything for our perfect happiness in heaven,
and if it takes my dog being there, I believe he'll be there."
Billy Graham

Additional copies of Mountain Mutts can be obtained from
Julie-Stephens.com

Mountain Mutts – Joy's Tale

Story and Photographs
by
Julie Stephens

Once there were two friends who loved each other very much.

Winter was older.

Spring was bigger.

Winter was the leader. Spring was the follower.

Wherever Winter went, Spring followed.

Spring did not remember a time when her beloved friend was not right there.

Spring

Winter

When Winter thought an almost empty peanut butter container was delicious…

…Spring wanted to try it too.

Winter and Spring
played frequently.

When Winter went
down to the river,
Spring followed.

Spring was so
contented, so happy
to snuggle with her
friend Winter.

Then one day…Winter died.

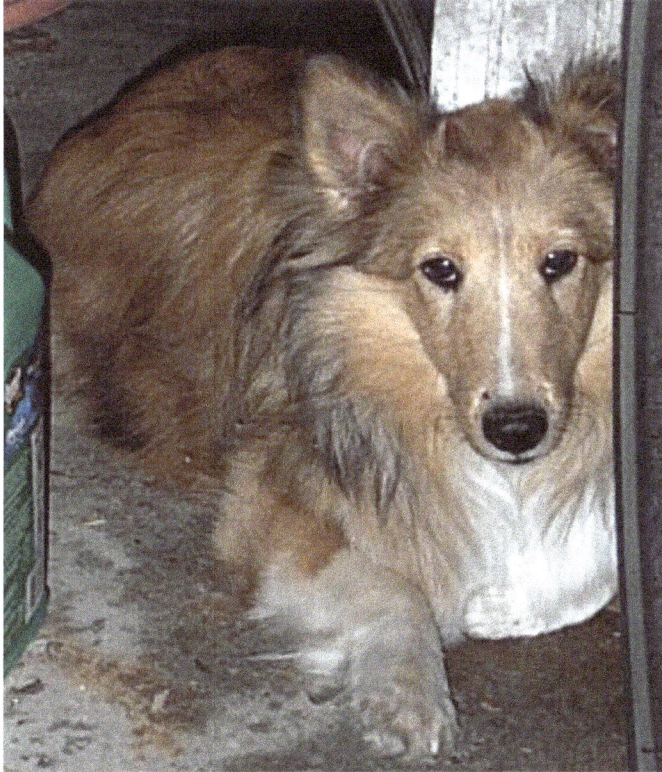

Spring was sad. She felt miserable. Winter was Spring's dearest friend, and Winter was gone. Spring was despondent.

Spring didn't have an appetite or energy to do anything. She didn't want an almost empty peanut butter container. She didn't want to play by the river. She missed snuggling with her friend.

The whole house was hushed with big sighs and tears. When Winter died, it was a sad, sad time for the whole family.
Day after day there was no joy

After a long time, the family couldn't cry or be sad anymore.
A puppy is what they needed.

The puppy's name will be Joy.
Yes! Joy is what the family needs.

This is Joy.

She is a little, tiny puppy with an enormous responsibility.
Spring needs her.

What Joy doesn't know yet, is that she needs Spring, too.

Joy tries to get Spring's attention. Spring ignores the puppy.

"Here, Spring! Here's my chew bone for you. Don't you like it? Take it Spring! It is great for chewing.

All right, I'll go away and leave you alone."

Spring is silent. She does not want Joy close to her. Spring remembers playing with her friend Winter.

She sighs. Spring is too sad to play with Joy

Puppies like to snuggle and play, but Spring is still sad.

Joy is left alone.

Patient Joy plays by herself and waits for Spring to feel better.

Joy is a baby dog, and babies need a lot of sleep.

Joy naps everywhere by herself and waits for Spring to be her friend.

Joy waits and waits.

She plays alone.

She naps alone.

Joy waits.

Joy waits all alone.

One day, Joy curls up to take a nap next to Spring.

Spring doesn't move away!

It's a new
day
in the
mountains!

Spring walks out
onto the deck and
contemplates the
marvelous
possibilities of the
new day!

Joy is concerned
about the stairs.
This is high for a
little puppy.

"Come on, Joy! You can do it!
There is a lot of exploring for us to do."

Spring runs off,
expecting her little companion to follow.

"I did it! I did it by myself!"

"What a great feeling! Yea! I went down the high stairs."

Joy saw Spring heading down to the river and ran after her friend. "Now where did Spring go? Spring isn't here. Oh my! What a mess I've gotten myself into! How do I get back on the soft grass?"

"Spring!

My friend!

My hero!"

Spring smiles!

Spring and Joy run and play together in the grass.

Spring shows Joy how to fetch a stick.

Spring prances down to her favorite place and shows Joy how to get a drink out of the river.

The cool water is delicious after chewing a dry stick.

The dogs wag their tails the way dogs do when they are happy!

Joy does not know it, but she has a broken tail. She was born that way.

Her tail will not straighten all the way out, or wag like most dogs.

Some would consider this a problem, but Spring and Joy do not pay any attention to Joy's bent tail.

Spring's tummy rumbled. "It's treat time, Joy! Let's go home and tell our people."

Joy didn't know yet, but every day about lunchtime, there would be a treat for the dogs.

"When our people have a treat for us, look up at them adoringly," Spring explains to Joy.

After treat time, the friends decide to take a nap together.

It is a peaceful time; filled with joy.

This story is just beginning.

About The Author

Though born below sea level in New Orleans, Julie now lives in the most remote area of the lower 48 states with her husband and their dogs at 9,000 feet above sea level. She is an award-winning photographer and writer with her newspaper column "Life From My View" and her picture book: **Mountain Mutts – Joy's Tale**.

Julie has a BFA in theater, has performed in community theater and a television commercial. She also has a Master's in Education and has taught just about every level from preschool to graduate school. She and her husband have a grown son and daughter and four grandchildren.

The Stephens delight in daily living with nature and walking the mountains with their dogs. Julie spends most of her unscheduled days reading, writing, and walking with her camera in hand. Her books are available on her website: **Julie-Stephens.com**

"The most precious gift we can give one another is letting them know they matter."
Julie A R Stephens

Hands Be Strong, Inc.

The Creation of Adam (detail) Michelangelo (1475-1564)

Additional copies of
Mountain Mutts - Joy's Tale
can be obtained from Julie-Stephens.com

A companion teacher's guide for **Mountain Mutts - Joy's Tale**
is available for free download at Julie-Stephens.com

Questions or comments about this material can be directed to:
support@handsbestrong.com

May the graciousness of the LORD our God be upon us;
prosper the work of our hands;
prosper our handiwork.   Psalm 90:17

www.ingramcontent.com/pod-product-compliance
Lightning Source LLC
Chambersburg PA
CBHW041600260326
41914CB00011B/1325